DRILL AND RIFLE INSTRUCTION

FOR THE

CORPS OF RIFLE VOLUNTEERS,

By Authority

OF

THE SECRETARY OF STATE FOR WAR.

SIXTH EDITION.

LONDON:

The Naval & Military Press Ltd

Published by the

The Naval & Military Press

in association with the Royal Armouries

Unit 10 Ridgewood Industrial Park,
Uckfield, East Sussex, TN22 5QE
Tel: +44 (0) 1825 749494
Fax: +44 (0) 1825 765701

MILITARY HISTORY AT YOUR FINGERTIPS
www.naval-military-press.com

ONLINE GENEALOGY RESEARCH
www.military-genealogy.com

ONLINE MILITARY CARTOGRAPHY
www.militarymaproom.com

ROYAL
ARMOURIES

The Library & Archives Department at the
Royal Armouries Museum, Leeds, specialises
in the history and development of armour
and weapons from earliest times to the
present day. Material relating to the
development of artillery and modern
fortifications is held at the Royal
Armouries Museum, Fort Nelson.

For further information contact:
Royal Armouries Museum, Library, Armouries Drive,
Leeds, West Yorkshire LS10 1LT
Royal Armouries, Library, Fort Nelson, Down End Road, Fareham PO17 6AN

Or visit the Museum's website at
www.armouries.org.uk

*In reprinting in facsimile from the original, any imperfections are inevitably reproduced
and the quality may fall short of modern type and cartographic standards.
Printed and bound by CPI Antony Rowe, Eastbourne*

PREFACE.

VOLUNTEERS having other occupations cannot be expected to devote many hours a-day to drill and rifle practice; under this consideration the Compiler has endeavoured to reduce the system explained in the following Manual to the simplest form.

He has restricted himself as nearly as possible to the movements and formations recommended by Sir Charles Napier, in his excellent "Letter on the Defence of England," and he strongly recommends all volunteers to follow the advice of that talented soldier,—

"Do not let any one persuade you to learn *more.*"

Volunteers thoroughly instructed in the few movements laid down in the following pages, which may be learned in a short space of time, will be far more efficient than those who attempt to acquire the more complicated system of drill detailed in the Field Exercise book for regular troops, in which, from the nature of their organization, they can never expect to arrive at any great degree of proficiency.

D. LYSONS, Colonel,
Assistant Adjutant-General.

CONTENTS.

FIFTH LESSON.

SIXTH LESSON.

ADDITIONAL INSTRUCTION.

INSTRUCTION OF MUSKETRY.

FORMS.

CIRCULAR.

4

The following Alterations have been made since the publication of the First Edition.

Page 23, line 9 from the bottom, *for* Load, *read* TWO.

Page 24, paragraph 4, *for*—

SHOULDER ARMS. { "1. *To Shoulder.*—Bring the left foot "back to the right, and turn," &c.,

read—

SHOULDER ARMS. { "1. *To Shoulder.*—At the word SHOULDER, bring the left foot back to the right. At the word ARMS, turn," &c.

Page 27, paragraph 1, *for* paragraph *substitute*—

" *To Shoulder and Order from the Capping Position kneeling.*

SHOULDER ARMS, or ORDER ARMS. { At the word SHOULDER or ORDER, spring up to the standing position, at the half face to the right, bringing the right heel to the left. At the word ARMS, proceed as described in the shouldering, or ordering from the capping position standing."

Page 51, lines 14 and 15, *for* 20 *read* 10.

INSTRUCTIONS FOR THE TRAINING

OF

VOLUNTEER CORPS.

GENERAL REMARKS.

1. VOLUNTEER corps will be composed, for the most part, of men whose time is much occupied with their ordinary pursuits, and who consequently will not be able to spare many hours for drill ; it is therefore recommended that every volunteer be provided with a copy of this drill book, in order that he may read the instructions between the drills, which will be found a great assistance.

2. The names of the different parts of the rifle, the way to clean it, and the theoretical principles, may be learned by studying the book. Occasional examinations by the musketry instructor will however be useful, to ascertain if the volunteers have properly understood what they have read.

3. When a corps of volunteers is first assembled, if there are no regular drill instructors attached to it, the commanding officer would do wisely at once to select, or cause to be selected, a certain number of the members, in the proportion of about 10 or 12 per cent., to act as such. These men may afterwards become non-commissioned officers, and rank according to the aptitude they show for military duties.

4. The volunteers thus selected should first be trained in a squad by themselves, after which they will be employed in drilling the remainder of the corps, and time will eventually be gained.

5. The corps being assembled, and the drill instructors ready to begin their work, the volunteers will be divided into as many squads as there are instructors, and each instructor will proceed with the following lessons.

6. The volunteers, when at drill, must remain perfectly silent, and give their whole attention to their instructors.

7. The volunteers should be perfect in one lesson, before they proceed to another ; each lesson may be repeated as often as it is found necessary, and time will permit.

8. A system of mutual instruction will frequently be found advantageous ; as the volunteers get more acquainted with their drill, each in succession may be called out, and directed to put the squad through one or two exercises, under the superintendence of the instructor.

FIRST LESSON.

Squad falling in.

The squad will fall in, in line, that is side by side. The right hand man being first placed, the remainder will then fall in one after the other, touching very lightly towards him ; the thick part of the arm just below the elbow is the part that should keep the touch, and will be the principal guide when marching.

Telling off.

The volunteers will number off from right to left, each man calling out his number thus,—" one," " two," " three," &c., the right hand man being " one."

It must be explained to them that odd numbers are called right files, even numbers left files.

Opening for Squad Drill.

In all the following exercises, the instructor will first give the word of command in the margin distinctly, in the ordinary tone of his voice, the volunteers remaining steady ; he will then explain to them, in the words of the text, the movement required. This done, he will repeat the word of command in a loud tone, the first or cautionary part, slowly and distinctly, the last, or executive word or syllable, on which the men will move as directed, sharply and decidedly.

PLATE I.

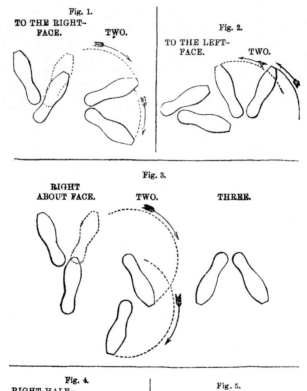

Fig. 1.
TO THE RIGHT-FACE.   TWO.

Fig. 2.
TO THE LEFT-FACE.   TWO.

Fig. 3.

RIGHT ABOUT FACE.   TWO.   THREE.

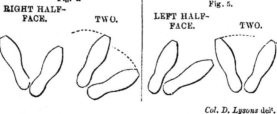

Fig. 4.
RIGHT HALF-FACE.   TWO.

Fig. 5.
LEFT HALF-FACE.   TWO.

Col. D. Lysons delt.

RIGHT FILES ONE PACE FORWARD, LEFT FILES ONE PACE STEP BACK— MARCH.

On the word MARCH, the right files will take one pace to the front, and the left files will take one pace to the rear, both with the left feet, and then stand perfectly still.

Position of the Volunteer.

The instructor will place each volunteer in his proper position as follows:—The shoulders square to the front, heels together, toes turned out, so that the feet may form an angle of 60 degrees, the arms hanging straight down from the shoulders, palms of the hands flat to the thighs, the body straight, but inclining forward, so that the weight of it may bear principally on the fore part of the feet, the head erect, but not thrown back, and the eyes looking straight to the front.

The above position should be perfectly easy and natural, without any stiffness or constraint.

Standing at Ease.

SQUAD, STAND AT— EASE.

On the words STAND AT EASE, bring the left foot about six inches to the front, the greater part of the weight of the body on the right leg, the left knee a little bent ; at the same time strike the palms of the hands together, and pass the right hand over the back of the left, letting them hang easily together in front of the body ; the whole position should be easy.

SQUAD— ATTENTION.

At the word ATTENTION, draw back the left foot, drop the hands to the sides, and resume the first position taught.

Facings.—Plate I.

In facing, the left heel never quits the ground, but the body turns on it as on a pivot, the right foot being drawn back to turn the body to the right, and carried forward to turn it to the left, as follows :—

TO THE RIGHT—FACE.	On the word FACE, place the hollow of the right foot smartly against the left heel, keeping the shoulders square to the front.
TWO.	On the word TWO, raise the toes, and turn a quarter circle to the right on both heels, which must be pressed together.
TO THE LEFT—FACE.	On the word FACE, place the right heel against the hollow of the left foot, keeping the shoulders square to the front.
TWO.	On the word TWO, raise the toes and turn a quarter circle to the left on both heels, which must be pressed together.
RIGHT ABOUT—FACE.	On the word FACE, place the ball of the right toe against the left heel, keeping the shoulders square to the front.
TWO.	On the word TWO, raise the toes and turn to the right about on both heels.
THREE.	On the word THREE, bring the right foot smartly back in a line with the left.
RIGHT (or LEFT) HALF—FACE.	On the word FACE, draw back (or advance) the right foot one inch.
TWO.	On the word TWO, raise the toes and turn an eighth of a circle to the right (or left) on both heels.

The volunteers will also be taught to face, judging their own time, that is, without the words TWO, or THREE, resting a pause of nearly a second between each movement.

| SQUAD—FRONT. | When it is intended to resume the original front, after any of the foregoing facings, the word of command FRONT, may be given, on which the whole will face, as accurately as possible, to their former front. |

Closing the Squad.

| RIGHT FILES— ONE PACE STEP BACK. LEFT FILES ONE PACE FORWARD— MARCH. | On the word MARCH, the right and left files will step as directed, with their left feet, thus resuming their original places in line. |

Dressing.

EYES RIGHT—
DRESS.

On the word EYES RIGHT, turn the head and eyes slightly to the right, and on the word DRESS, shuffle up or back with very short steps, till you can just see the lower part of the face of the second man from you ; at the same time, touch very lightly towards the flank on which you are dressing.

In like manner volunteers will be taught to dress by the left.

These practices should be repeated several times, after which the volunteers will be dismissed, in the following manner.

Dismissing a Squad.

STAND AT—
EASE.

As already explained.

BREAK OFF.

On this word the volunteers will disperse quietly.

To save time, the volunteers should be warned, previously to being dismissed, when and how they are to fall in for the next drill.

SECOND LESSON.

The squad will fall in, and tell off as at the first lesson, but will remain in single rank, in which order they will first practise the facings, judging their own time, and will then learn to march in quick and double time.

Marching.

It will not be necessary to teach volunteers to march accurately in regular cadence, in the rigid manner that soldiers of the line are taught, but a little practice in the quick and double march will be useful to enable them to advance together in line ; they will also find it less fatiguing when marching a distance if they keep step.

The length of the pace in the quick march is 30 inches, in the double march 36.

The time or cadence is, in the quick march 108 steps in a minute, in the double march 150.

BY THE RIGHT (or LEFT).	On the words, BY THE RIGHT, or BY THE LEFT, remain steady ; it is simply to warn you which flank is to direct during the march. The man on the named flank will take two points, such as stones or tufts of grass, one beyond the other, straight to his front to march on, and as he approaches the nearest point, when marching, he will select a fresh one further off, so that he will always have two to keep him straight ; the remainder of the squad will touch very lightly towards him.

Before the squad is put in motion the time should be beaten on a drum ;* when the drum ceases, the instructor will at once give his command.

QUICK-MARCH.	On the word MARCH, step off together with the left foot, keeping the time given on the drum as nearly as possible. While marching, retain the position already taught, the body inclining well forward ; let the arms and hands hang easily, neither clinging to the thighs nor partaking of their movements.

HALT.	On the word HALT, complete the pace you are in the act of making, bring the heels together, and then stand still.

The volunteers should not be halted if they lose step, but be allowed to move on some distance.

RIGHT ABOUT— FACE. BY THE RIGHT (or LEFT) QUICK— MARCH.	The squad will then be faced about, and marched back again.

* To enable the drummer to beat the time correctly, a pendulum should be used ; a variety of instruments are constructed for this purpose, but a leaden plummet, suspended by a string that is not liable to stretch, will do as well. The length from the point of suspension to the centre of the plummet must be as follows :—

		Inches.	Hundredths.
Quick time	- - - - - - -	12	93
Double time	- - - - - - -	6	26

PLATE II.

KEY TO PLATES.

CAPTAIN..... .... Covering-Serjeant ... .

LIEUTENANT .... Serjeant ....

ENSIGN....... .... PRIVATES { Front rank .... Rear rank.. ....

FORMER POSITION......

Fig. 1.

THE DIAGONAL MARCH.

TO THE RIGHT HALF FACE QUICK MARCH. HALT-FRONT.

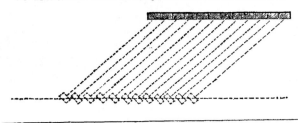

Fig. 2.

FORM RALLYING SQUARES.

HALT–FRONT.	As already taught.
RIGHT ABOUT– TURN.	The volunteers should also be taught to turn to the right about while marching. The turn should be completed in three short steps. The fourth must be a full pace in the new direction.

Stepping Out and Stepping Short and Marking Time.

Although 30 inches is the regular pace in quick time, a man may occasionally find it necessary to lengthen or shorten his pace in order to conform with the movements of the rest of the squad ; he may also mark the time by raising the feet alternately, without gaining ground.

File Marching.

Volunteers should never be required to march any distance in files, in close order, except when extending from " the Halt ;" it is not therefore necessary for them to attain great accuracy in this difficult movement.

TO THE RIGHT (or LEFT)– FACE.	As already described.
QUICK–MARCH.	On the word MARCH, step off together with the left feet, one behind the other. In this march you must keep step, and take care to step off at once at a full pace.
HALT—FRONT.	On the words HALT—FRONT, halt and face to the original front.

The Diagonal March.—Plate II., fig. 1.

The men will first be taught the diagonal march from the halt, then on the march.

RIGHT (or LEFT) HALF– FACE.	As already taught.
QUICK– MARCH.	On the word MARCH, step off, each man moving straight to his front and retaining during the march, his relative position with the rest of the squad.
HALT–FRONT.	As already described.

If the march has been properly performed, when the squad is halted and fronted, it will be found in a line parallel to its original position.

BY THE RIGHT (or LEFT) QUICK—MARCH.	As already described.
RIGHT (or LEFT) HALF—TURN.	On the word TURN, each volunteer will turn his body the eighth of a circle to the right (or left), as directed, and move on in a diagonal direction, without checking the pace.
FRONT—TURN BY THE RIGHT (or LEFT.)	On the word TURN, turn to the front and move on in line to the original front.

If the squad inclines to a flank in this manner while retiring, and is required again to move straight to the rear, the word will be REAR TURN.

When marching diagonally to the right, the right file will direct, when to the left, the left file will direct, without reference to the flank that was previously directing.

Breaking off and Re-assembling.

STAND AT—EASE. FOR A FEW MOMENTS ONLY, BREAK OFF.	As already taught.
FALL IN.	On the word FALL IN, the squad will fall in at once in the places they previously occupied.

This should be done frequently ; it is a very important practice.

The Double March.

The time will first be given on the drum.

BY THE RIGHT (or LEFT,) DOUBLE—MARCH.	On the word MARCH, step off with a good long swinging step (36 inches), the body well forward, and carried smoothly to the front, shoulders square, the whole position easy and elastic.
HALT.	As in quick time.

Wheeling.

RIGHT WHEEL
QUICK-MARCH.
> On the word MARCH, the right-hand man will mark time, moving his shoulders round as the squad wheels round him ; the remainder of the men will wheel round the right or pivot man, touching towards him and looking outwards for the dressing. The left-hand or outward man will move at a full pace of 30 inches and look inwards.

HALT.
or
FORWARD,
BY THE RIGHT
(or LEFT.)
> On the word HALT, the squad will halt, and every man will look to his front ; or if the word FORWARD is given, it will move on in the direction it happens to be facing when the word is given.

Wheeling to the left will be practised in like manner ; a squad may also wheel in any direction while on the march, by the words RIGHT (or LEFT) WHEEL, on which the pivot man will mark time, and the wheel will be performed as already explained.

Before dismissing the squad, when this lesson is perfect, the volunteers should be warned to assemble the next time with their rifles in their hands.

THIRD LESSON.

Manual Exercise.

This drill applies equally to corps armed with the long and short rifle.

The volunteers will fall in as usual, with their rifles in their right hands, and will first be taught to stand with their arms at the shoulder as follows :—

The rifle when at the SHOULDER is to be carried in the right hand at the full extent of the arm, close to the side ; guard to the front, with the forefinger and thumb round it, the remaining fingers under the cock ; the upper part of the barrel close in to the hollow of the shoulder.

They will then be taught the following movements :—

ORDER—ARMS.
> Seize the rifle with the left hand, thumb and fingers round the piece, the little finger in line with the point of the right shoulder, but without moving the barrel therefrom, arm close to the body.

TWO.

Slip the rifle down with the left hand as low as the left arm will admit, keeping the arm and rifle close to the body, and with the right hand, which is to seize the rifle between the bands, place the butt quietly on the ground even with the toe of the right foot, bringing the left hand at the same instant to the left side ; the right arm to be slightly bent, the thumb round the barrel, pressed against the thigh, fingers slanting towards the ground.

FIX-SWORDS.

Place the rifle with the right hand between the knees, guard to the front, then draw the sword with the right hand, holding the scabbard with the left, turn the point upwards, and seize the rifle with the left hand at the "nose cap," then place the back part of the handle of the sword against the lock side of the barrel, knuckles to the right, arm close to the body, and slide the spring on to the catch, and the ring on to the muzzle ; when this is done, seize the rifle with the right hand between the bands, bring the left hand to the left side, and come to the position of "order arms."

SHOULDER-ARMS.

Raise the rifle with a smart jerk of the right hand, and seize it as described in the position "at the shoulder ;" at the same time seize the rifle also with the left hand in line with the elbow to steady it in the shoulder, arm close to the body.

TWO.

Bring the left hand to the left side.

PRESENT ARMS.

Seize the rifle with the left hand at the lower band, raising it a few inches by slightly bending the right arm, but without moving the barrel from the shoulder, and slip the thumb of the right hand under the cock, bringing the fingers under the guard to the front, and slanting downwards ; both arms close to the body ; left hand square with the left elbow.

TWO.	Raise the rifle with the right hand perpendicularly from the shoulder to the *poise*, bringing it in front of the centre of the body, lock to the front ; at the same time place the left hand smartly on the stock with the fingers pointing upwards, the thumb close to the forefinger, the point in line with the mouth, the wrist on the trigger guard, the left elbow close to the butt, the right elbow and butt close to the body.
THREE.	Bring the rifle down with a quick motion as low as the right hand will admit without constraint, guard to the front, and grasp it with the left hand, the little finger touching the projection above the lock plate, thumb between stock and barrel, at the same time draw back the right foot so that the hollow of it may touch the left heel ; lightly holding the small of the butt with the right hand, fingers pointing rather downwards ; the rifle in this position to be totally supported with the left hand, close in front of and opposite the centre of the body.
SHOULDER, ARMS.	Bring the rifle to the right side, and seize it with the right hand, the thumb and forefinger round the guard at the full extent of the arm, remaining fingers under the cock, bringing the left hand square with the left elbow and the right foot to its original position, both arms close to the body.
TWO.	Bring the left hand smartly to the left side.
SLOPE—ARMS.	The same as the first motion of "Present Arms."
TWO.	Bring the rifle on to the left shoulder, muzzle slanting to the rear, and seize it with the left hand, the first two joints of the fingers grasping the butt, thumb alone on the heel of it, the guard pressed gently against the shoulder, left elbow close to the side.
THREE.	Bring the right hand down to the right side.

CARRY–ARMS.	Seize the small of the butt with the right hand.
TWO.	Bring the rifle to the right side and seize it as described in the position "at the shoulder," carrying the left hand across the body to steady it.
THREE.	Drop the left arm to the left side.
PORT–ARMS.	The same as the first motion of "Present Arms."
TWO.	Bring the rifle in the left hand to a diagonal position across the body, lock to the front, and seize the small of the butt at once with the right hand, thumb and fingers round the stock, the left wrist to be opposite the left breast, both elbows close to the body, the muzzle slanting upwards, so that the barrel may cross opposite the point of the left shoulder.
CHARGE–SWORDS.	Make a right half-face, the right toes to point to the right, the left full to the front, and bring down the rifle to nearly a horizontal position at the right side, with the muzzle inclining a little upwards, the right wrist to rest against the hollow of the thigh below the hip, the thumb of the right hand pointing to the muzzle.

Whenever a company in line charges with swords, the whole are in the first instance to advance in quick time with shouldered arms; at the command PREPARE TO CHARGE, the rifles of the front rank will be brought to the long trail, and those of the rear rank to the slope; at the word CHARGE, the rifles of the front rank will be brought to the charging position, and the pace increased to the double march, carefully avoiding too much hurry. On the word HALT, both ranks will halt and shoulder arms.

SHOULDER–ARMS.	Raise the rifle to a perpendicular position at the right side, and seize it with the right hand as described in the position "at the shoulder," the left hand holding the piece above the lower band square with the left elbow, both arms close to the body.

TWO.	Bring the left hand to the left side.
ORDER–ARMS.	As already detailed.

UNFIX–SWORDS.
> Place the rifle with the right hand between the knees, guard to the front, seize it with the left hand at the "nose cap," and seize the handle of the sword with the right hand, knuckles to front, fingers pointing downwards ; then with the forefinger press the spring inwards, raise the sword upwards, and drop the point, with the edge to the front, towards the scabbard, raising the right elbow in so doing, at the same time seize the top of the scabbard with the left hand, to guide the sword into it. Return the sword, and bring the rifle with the right hand to the "order."

TRAIL–ARMS.
> Bring the rifle to a horizontal position at the right side, holding it with the right hand behind the lower band (thumb and fingers round the piece) at the full extent of the arm.

SHOULDER–ARMS.
> Raise the rifle to a perpendicular position at the right side, and seize it with the right hand as described in the position "at the shoulder," the left hand holding the piece above the lower band square with the left elbow, both arms close to the body.

TWO.
> Bring the left hand to the left side.

TRAIL–ARMS.
> Seize the rifle with the left hand, little finger in line with the elbow, arm close to the body.

TWO.
> Raise the right hand and seize the rifle below the lower band, thumb and fingers round it ; then bring the rifle down to a horizontal position at the full extent of the arm, and at the same time bring the left hand to the left side.

ORDER–ARMS.
> Bring the rifle to a perpendicular position at the right side, placing the butt quietly on the ground, and come to the position of "order arms,"

B

STAND AT–
EASE.
> Push the muzzle of the rifle to the front with the right hand, arm close to the side, at the same time move the left foot six inches to the front, the knee slightly bent, and the principal weight of the body resting on the right leg, as described in lesson 1.

Volunteers will also be taught these movements, judging their own time, in the same manner as they have been taught the facings.

The volunteers will then be practised, with their arms, in marching and turning, in quick and double time. In turning to the right about with trailed arms, they will bring the rifle to a perpendicular position on the first step of the turn, and trail again on the fourth.

When moving with trailed arms, at the word HALT, arms are to be ordered, and when the men are at the halt, on the words QUICK or DOUBLE MARCH being given, arms are to be trailed, as they step off, without any command to that effect.

In ordering arms from any position, the greatest care is to be taken to prevent the rifle falling on, or striking the ground, and it is not to be unnecessarily shaken in performing any of the motions of the manual exercise.

Method of Piling Arms.

For this practice the squad will be formed in two ranks, the rear rank a pace and a half (45 inches) from the front rank, measuring from the heels of one rank to the heels of the other. It will then be told off from right to left.

PILE–ARMS.
> At the word PILE, the front rank will draw back their right feet in order to face to the right about ; at the word ARMS, the front rank will face about, bringing their rifles with them to ordered arms ; the whole will then place the butts of their rifles between their feet, locks from them, barrels to the right, after which the right file rear rank and the left file front rank will incline their rifles towards each other, and cross ramrods. The front rank man of the right file will then seize the rifle of the front

rank man of the left file, with his left hand, round the muzzle, bearing it from him, and with the right hand he will pass his own ramrod between the ramrods and muzzles of the two firelocks already crossed ; the left file rear rank will then lodge his rifle between the muzzles of the rifles of the front rank, sling uppermost. When there is an odd file, that is a right file without a left file, each man of the file will lodge his rifle against the pile nearest his right hand.

STAND CLEAR. Ranks take a pace of ten inches backwards and face towards the pivot flank.

STAND TO. Ranks facing towards the pivot flank, will face inwards and close on their arms by taking a pace of ten inches forward.

UNPILE-ARMS. At the word UNPILE, seize the rifle with the right hand under the top band, front rank at the same time drawing back their right feet in order to face to the right about ; at the word ARMS, unlock the ramrods without hurry, by inclining the butts inwards, and come to ordered arms, the front rank will then *front*.

It is necessary to be careful in piling and unpiling arms to prevent damage being done to the ramrods and sights.

When there is an odd file, it must always be the third from the left of the squad or company, which will bring two right files together, the second being an even number and its left file (the left file of the squad) an odd number.

FOURTH LESSON.

Platoon Exercise by Numbers.

AS A FRONT (or REAR) RANK. PREPARE TO LOAD. 1. *From the shoulder.*—Seize the rifle as described in the first movement of " order " arms," and make a half face to the right, left toes pointing to the front, right toes to the right, eyes to the front.

As a front rank.—Carry the left foot ten inches to the left front in a diagonal direction, carrying the body with it. *As a*

TWO. { *rear rank.*—Carry the left foot six inches to the front, moving the body with it, shoulders to be square to the front ; bring the rifle down in the left hand, and place the butt quietly on the ground against the inside of the left foot, barrel to the front ; at the same time slip up the left hand, and seize the rifle round the nose cap, thumb pointing to the muzzle, arm close to the side : carry the right hand at once to the pouch, take up a cartridge, holding it with the forefinger and thumb close to the top, with the bullet in the palm of the hand.

LOAD. { Bring the cartridge to the forefinger and thumb of the left hand, and carefully tear off the end without spilling the powder, then replace the finger and thumb as before.

TWO. { Bring the cartridge to the muzzle, and pour the powder into the barrel, turning the elbow up, and palm of the hand to the front.

THREE. { Reverse the cartridge by turning the knuckles to the front, and put the bullet in the barrel nearly as far as the top, still holding the paper close above the bullet, elbow up.

FOUR. { By a turn of the wrist from left to right, and dropping the elbow, tear off the paper, and then seize the head of the ramrod between the forefinger and thumb, knuckles towards the body.

ROD. { Force the ramrod up and seize it in the middle between the first two fingers and thumb, knuckles towards the body, elbow as high as the wrist.

TWO. { Draw the ramrod straight out, turn it over towards the front, and place the head of it on the bullet, still holding the ramrod with the two first fingers and the thumb, the remaining fingers closed in the hand, knuckles to the front, elbow near to the ramrod, shoulders square.

HOME. { Force the bullet down till the second finger touches the barrel, bringing the elbow close to the body.

TWO.
> Slip the right hand up to the point of the ramrod, and force the bullet steadily to the bottom.

THREE.
> By two firm pressures, raising the ramrod about one inch on each occasion, ascertain that the bullet is resting on the powder ; all strokes which may indent the point of the bullet to be avoided.

RETURN.
> Draw up the ramrod and seize it in the middle as in the first motion of the "rod."

TWO.
> Draw the ramrod straight out, turn it over, the point towards the front, and put it into its place, pressing it towards the body in so doing to prevent the point catching the band, raise the right hand, place the second joint of the forefinger on the head of the ramrod and force it home ; then seize it between the second joint of the forefinger and thumb, and slip the left hand down at the same instant to its full extent and seize the rifle.

CAP.
> Turn the shoulders and body a half face to the right without moving the feet, bring the rifle to the right side, in a horizontal position, with the left hand, which will grasp it behind the lower band, thumb between stock and barrel ; at the same time meet the small of the butt with the right-hand, fingers behind the trigger guard, half cock the rifle with the thumb, left arm close to the body. *As a front rank*, the small of the butt must be pressed against the hip ; *as a rear rank*, four inches above it.

TWO.
> Throw off the old cap with the right hand, then take a new one from the cap pocket, put it on the nipple, and press it home with the thumb. Then bring the hand to the "small" of the butt, and hold it lightly with the fingers behind the trigger-guard, thumb pointing to the muzzle.

AT — YDS.
READY.

Carry the right hand to the sight, and with the forefinger and thumb adjust the sliding bar, placing the top even with the line, or to the place that indicates the elevation necessary for the distance named; then raise the flap without a jerk, from the top, if required; after which bring the hand back to the small of the butt, and full cock the rifle, and hold it lightly with the fingers behind the trigger guard, thumb pointing to the muzzle, and fix the eye stedfastly on some object in front.

PRESENT.

Bring the rifle to the shoulder, carrying it well to the front, so as to clear the body as it goes up, keeping a firm hold of it behind the lower band with the left hand; raise the right elbow as high as the shoulder and a little forward; press the butt against the shoulder with the left hand, and bring the left elbow well under the rifle to form a support : hold the butt lightly with the right hand, the muzzle pointing a few inches below the object which the eye is fixed on, the forefinger along the outside of the trigger guard, and the left eye closed.

It is very important that the volunteer be well practised in bringing his rifle to the " Present," the instructor will therefore cause him frequently to repeat the motion as above described, directing him to bring the rifle down again to the right side at the words, AS YOU WERE.

TWO.

Place the forefinger round the trigger like a hook, that part of it between the first and second joint to rest flat on the trigger, and restrain the breathing.

THREE.

Raise the muzzle steadily until the top of the fore-sight is brought in a line with the object through the bottom of the notch of the back-sight.

FOUR.

Press the trigger without the least jerk or motion of the hand, eye, or arm until the cock falls upon the nipple, keeping the eye still firmly fixed upon the object.

FIVE. ⎰ Bring the rifle to the capping position, and shut down the flap, but without moving the sliding bar, and immediately seize the rifle with the right hand close in front of the left, fore arm close to the barrel ; and after a pause, taking the time from the right, turn the barrel at once downwards, and bring the rifle to a perpendicular position opposite the right breast in the right hand, then seize it with the left hand at the nose cap, and come to the position of " prepare to load," 2nd motion.

The volunteer should always be taught to aim at some positive object when bringing his rifle to the " Present ;" for this purpose small bulls'-eyes should be painted on a wall or fence one above another, two and four feet from the ground, and at lateral distances of three feet ; they should be white, the size of a crown piece, with black centres the size of a shilling.

Particular attention is to be given to the following points, in the " Present," the body is to be firm and upright, the butt to be pressed firmly into the hollow of the shoulder, the rifle to be held firmly in the left hand, the sight to be upright, and in aiming, the muzzle to be steadily raised, until the top of the fore-sight is aligned upon the object on which the right eye is fixed, through the bottom of the notch of the back-sight, the left eye being closed and the breathing restrained. In delivering the fire, the trigger is to be moved by pressure alone, without any motion of the hand, eye, or elbow ; the right eye to continue fixed on the object after snapping, to ascertain if the aim has been deranged by the movement of the trigger or body.

2. *From the Order.*—When required to load from the " Order," on the words PREPARE TO LOAD, the volunteer will make a half face to the right, as in loading from the shoulder, moving his rifle with the body. On the word TWO, he will bring his rifle with the right hand to the loading position, seizing it at the nose cap with the left hand ; in all other respects he will proceed as already described.

To come to the " Ready."

AS A FRONT (or REAR) RANK ⎰ 1. *From the Shoulder.*—Make a right half face, the left foot to point to the front, the right foot to the right, at the same

AT — YARDS.
READY.

time seize the rifle with the left hand, the little finger in line with the right elbow.

TWO.

Bring the rifle to a horizontal position at the right side, grasping it firmly with the left hand behind the lower band, thumb between the stock and barrel, left arm close to the body ; *as a front rank* the small of the butt must be pressed against the hip ; *as a rear rank*, four inches above it. Then carry the left foot, *as a front rank*, ten inches to the left front in a diagonal direction, carrying the body with it ; *as a rear rank*, six inches to the front, moving the body with it, and proceed as already described in the "Ready," page 22.

AS A FRONT
or REAR RANK
AT — YARDS.
READY.

2. *From the Order.*—Make a right half face as before described, carrying the rifle round with the body.

TWO.

Bring the rifle to a horizontal position at the right side, grasping it with the left hand, and proceed as above described.

To Shoulder and Order from the Capping Position.

SHOULDER
ARMS.

1. *To Shoulder.*—At the word SHOUL-DER, bring the left foot back to the right. At the word ARMS, turn upon the heels to the front, at the same time bring the rifle to its place at the shoulder, seizing it with the right hand.

TWO.

Drop the left hand to the side.

ORDER ARMS.

2. *To Order.*—At the word "ORDER," bring the left foot back to the right, and seize the rifle with the right hand close in front of the left ; fore-arm close to the barrel. At the word ARMS, face to the front, and with the right hand place the butt quietly on the ground, and drop the left arm to the left side, in the position at ordered arms, explained in the manual exercise.

To Fire and Re-load Kneeling.

FIRE AS A FRONT (or REAR) RANK KNEELING. AT — YARDS READY.	Sink down on the right knee; *as a front rank*, the knee should be 6 inches to the right, and 12 to the rear of the left heel; *as a rear rank*, 12 inches to the right and 12 to the rear of the left heel; the right foot upright and under the body, body resting on the heel, the lower part of the left leg nearly perpendicular, at the same time bring the rifle down to the ready position, adjust the sight, and cock as already described.
PRESENT.	As when standing, except that the left elbow is placed on the knee to form a support, the weight of the body still on the right foot.
TWO. THREE. FOUR.	As already explained when standing,

FIVE.

Front Rank.	Rear Rank.
Bring the rifle down to the capping position, at the same time raise the body off the right heel, and place the left fore-arm square on the left thigh six inches behind the knee; then shut down the flap without a jerk, and return the hand to the small of the butt. After a pause come to the position of "prepare to load," by carrying the rifle in both hands round in front of the left leg, turning the barrel downwards at the same time, and with the left hand passing the butt close by the body over the right heel to the left rear to the extent of the left arm, meeting it at the same time with the right hand, the	Bring the rifle down to the capping position, at the same time raise the body off the right heel, and place the left fore-arm square on the left knee; then shut down the flap without a jerk, and return the hand to the small of the butt; and after a pause come to the position of "prepare to load," by turning the rifle over in the left hand and placing the butt on the ground, lock uppermost, under the shin of the right leg of the front-rank man of the file on the right, meeting the barrel with the right-hand thumb in line with the muzzle, which is to be as high and in a line with the right shoulder, pointing

	Front Rank.	*Rear Rank.*

thumb in line with the muzzle, then seize the rifle with the left hand at the nose cap, afterwards carry the right hand to the pouch and proceed as already described. | to the rear, then seize the rifle with the left hand at the nose cap, afterwards carry the right hand to the pouch, and proceed as already described.

LOAD.
ONE.
TWO.
THREE.
FOUR.

} As already explained when standing. | As already explained when standing.

CAP.

With the left hand raise the butt over the right heel, close by the body, in a slanting direction, until the left elbow is brought in front of the hip, at the same time dropping the right hand to the right side, then bring the rifle round in front of the left leg, to a horizontal position at the right side, and the shoulders to the right half-face, placing the left fore-arm at once square on the thigh six inches behind the knee, and meeting the small of the butt with the right hand, which is to hold it lightly, with the fingers behind the trigger guard, and half cock the rifle, the thumb to remain on the cock ; the rifle to be grasped with the left hand, as detailed when capping standing ; the butt to be pressed against the side.

With the left hand bring the rifle to a horizontal position at the right side, muzzle to the front, and let the body resume the right half-face, place the left fore-arm at once square on the left knee, at the same time meet the small of the butt with the right hand, and hold it lightly with the fingers behind the guard, and half cock the rifle, the thumb to remain on the cock ; the rifle to be grasped with the left hand, as detailed when capping standing ; the butt to be pressed against the side.

TWO. As detailed when capping standing.

To Shoulder and Order from the Capping Position, kneeling.

SHOULDER
ARMS,
or
ORDER ARMS.

At the word SHOULDER, spring up to the standing position, at the half-face to the right, bringing the right heel to the left; at the word ORDER, spring up in like manner, and at the same time seize the rifle with the right hand close in front of the left. At the word ARMS, proceed as described in shouldering or ordering from the capping position standing.

Platoon Exercise in Slow and Quick Time.

The platoon exercise should first be taught by numbers, as detailed, then in slow time, that is, only repeating the cautions and commands thus :—PLATOON EXERCISE IN SLOW TIME. AS A FRONT (or REAR) RANK. PREPARE TO LOAD. LOAD. ROD. HOME. RETURN. CAP. FIRE A VOLLEY AT ———— YARDS. READY. PRESENT. After which the volunteers will be taught to load in quick time, that is, on the word LOAD, they will go through all the motions, and when loaded and capped they will wait at half-cock, at the capping position, for further orders.

FIFTH LESSON.

Formation of Squad in Two Ranks.

Three or four squads will now fall in together with shouldered arms in two ranks or lines, one behind the other, at one pace and a half (45 inches) from each other, measuring from the heels of the front rank to the heels of the rear rank.

Telling off.

The squad will tell off as usual, the front-rank men, only, calling out the numbers; but the rear-rank men equally attending to and remembering them.

If there is a man less in the rear rank than in the front rank, the man without a rear-rank man, called the blank file, will invariably be the third man from the left of the front rank.

28

The volunteers will be practised in the manual and platoon exercise, as already taught, in two ranks. Before loading or firing, the rear-rank men will, on the caution, invariably take a pace of 24 inches to the front, so as to lock up close to the front rank; and after they cease firing and are loaded the rear-rank men will take a pace to the rear, to resume their proper distance; they must also practise marching in quick and double time, turning about, and the diagonal march, the rear rank preserving its proper distance, and covering in rear of the front rank.

Firings.

The volunteers must also be practised in firing volleys by word of command, and in independent file firing, as follows :—

1. *Volleys.*

FIRE A VOLLEY. { On this caution the rear rank will close up as above directed.

AT—YARDS READY. } As already taught in the platoon exercise.

PRESENT. As already taught.

2. *File firing.*

FILE FIRING FROM THE RIGHT (or LEFT) OT FROM BOTH FLANKS. } On this caution the rear rank will close up, as above described.

COMMENCE FIRING. { On this word the flank file will make ready and fire, front-rank man first, rear-rank man immediately afterwards; they will then load; as the flank file comes to the present the next file will make ready, and so on for the first round, after which the files will fire and load independently. When only a few men are firing in the same direction, they must fire the first round very slowly, each file waiting till the file next to it is nearly reloaded; but when the whole corps is firing in one line the men may fire rather faster.

CEASE FIRING. { On this word each file will complete its loading, and " shoulder arms ;" if any man has " made ready," he will half cock his rifle ; the rear rank men will resume their proper distance as they shoulder.

As a general rule it will be advisable, when firing volleys or file firing, to direct the front rank to fire kneeling.

Skirmishing.

The volunteers will next be taught the following movements, which are necessary in skirmishing:—

An intelligent man should be placed in the centre of the squad for these movements.

Extending from the Halt.

In extending, as a general rule, it is the business of the rear rank man of each file to regulate the distance, and of the front rank man to look to the direction.

The number of paces that files are to extend from each other may be specified in the caution by the commander thus:—THREE PACES FROM THE RIGHT—EXTEND. When no number is specified, six paces will be the regulated distance between files.

A squad may be extended from the right file, left file, or centre file, or from any other named file.

FROM THE RIGHT, (LEFT, CENTRE, or N° — FILE)— EXTEND. { On the word EXTEND, the file on the named flank, or the centre or named file, will kneel down, the remainder will shoulder arms, face outwards, and extend in quick time.

The front rank men will move direct to the flank, covering correctly on the march, the rear-rank men will cast their eyes over the inward shoulder, and tap their respective front-rank men, as a signal to halt, front, and kneel, when they have gained their proper distances.

Closing on the Halt.

ON THE RIGHT (LEFT, CENTRE, or Nº—FILE)– CLOSE.

> On the word CLOSE, the file on the named flank, or the centre or named file, will rise, order arms, and stand at ease; the remainder will rise, face towards it, and close at quick time, halting, fronting, ordering arms, and standing at ease, in succession, as they arrive at their places.

The file on which the skirmishers close may be faced in any direction ; the remainder will form upon it, facing in the same direction.

Extending on the March.

FROM THE RIGHT (LEFT, CENTRE, or Nº — FILE)– EXTEND.

> On the word EXTEND, the file on the named flank, or the centre or named file, will continue to move straight forward in quick time; the remainder will make a half turn from the flank from which they are ordered to extend, and move off in double time. As soon as each file has extended to its proper distance, it will turn to its front and resume the quick time, the rear-rank men covering their front-rank men, and the whole keeping in line with the directing file.

When a company, extending on the march, is halted before all the files are extended, the remainder will make a second half turn outwards into file, break into quick time, shoulder arms, and complete their extension as from the halt.

Closing on the March..

ON THE RIGHT (LEFT, CENTRE, or Nº—FILE)– CLOSE.

> On the word CLOSE, the file on the named flank, or the centre or named file, will move steadily on in quick time ; the remainder will make a half turn towards it and close in double time, turning to the front and resuming the quick time as they arrive at their places.

When a company, closing on the march, is halted before all the files are closed, the remainder will make a second half turn inwards into file, break into quick time, and complete the formation as from the halt.

Advancing in Skirmishing Order.

COMPANY—
ADVANCE.

{ On the word ADVANCE, the volunteers will rise and step off in quick time, with trailed arms, keeping their distances from the centre.

Retiring in Skirmishing Order.

COMPANY—
RETIRE.

{ On the word RETIRE, the volunteers will rise, face to the right about, and step off in quick time, rear-rank in front, keeping their distances from the centre.

Volunteers in extended order will invariably face or turn to the right about, whether they are advancing, retiring, firing, or not firing.

Inclining to a Flank.

TO THE RIGHT
(or LEFT)—
INCLINE.

ADVANCE,
or
RETIRE.

{ On the word INCLINE, the skirmishers will make a half turn to the flank to which they are ordered to incline, and move in a diagonal direction, until they are ordered to resume their original direction to the front or rear, by the word of command ADVANCE or RETIRE. If the skirmishers have made a half turn, and are again ordered to incline in the same direction, on the second word INCLINE, they will complete the turn by making a second half turn, and will take ground to the flank in file.

HALT.

{ On the word HALT, when volunteers are inclining, they halt, front, and kneel.

When inclining to the right, the right file directs ; when inclining to the left, the left file directs. On the word ADVANCE OR RETIRE, the centre file resumes the direction.

Skirmishers changing Front or Direction.

1. *From the Halt.*—A line of skirmishers halted, can change front on any two named files that may be placed as a base for the rest to form upon.

A change of front in this manner may be made at any angle.

CHANGE FRONT TO THE RIGHT (or LEFT) ON THE TWO RIGHT (or LEFT) FILES.	On the caution the two named files will rise, and the instructor will dress them in the direction required ; as soon as they are placed they will again kneel.
DOUBLE-MARCH.	On the word MARCH, the whole will rise, and if all the files are to be thrown forward on a flank, they will make a half-face inwards, and run across by the shortest way to their places in the new line, dressing on the two base files, as they successively halt, and then kneeling.

If all the files are to be thrown back on either flank, they will turn round, move across, and halt, front, and kneel successively as they arrive at their places in the new line.

If the change is on two central files, part of the company will be thrown forward and the rest back, as above described.

SKIRMISHERS. RIGHT (or LEFT) WHEEL.	2. *On the March.* A line of skirmishers on the march may change its direction gradually, on the same principle as a company wheels when in close order. On the word WHEEL, the pivot file will halt, and the remainder will circle round it, the front-rank men looking outwards for the dressing, and the rear-rank men keeping the distances from the pivot flank.
FORWARD.	On the word FORWARD, the whole line will advance by the centre in the new direction.

Firing in Skirmishing Order.

The men of a file must always work together ; both men should never be unloaded at the same time ; they will fire alternately, commencing with the front-rank man. On broken ground the volunteers must take advantage of all cover, and when advancing or retiring they will run from one place of cover to another, the two men of each file keeping together and taking care not to get in the way of other files. When moving, the loaded man should always be nearest to the enemy.

The Rallying Square.—Plate II., fig. 2.

The instructor will place an officer or man as a rallying point in front of the squad, facing the supposed enemy. He will then call out any two men from the ranks, and direct them to fall in on the right and left of the rallying point, facing outwards ; then three more men, who will form in front of those posted, facing to the front ; then three more, who will form in rear of them, facing to the rear. The instructor will next cause four men to take post at the four angles, and others to complete the different faces of the square, and so on, till all the men are formed. Each man as he moves to his place will fix his sword. After this, the squad will be dispersed, and the rallying point being placed, the volunteers will be ordered to form rallying square, on which they will run in, and form as above described : the great object is to form a compact mass as quickly as possible ; provided the volunteers crowd close together round the rallying point, and face outwards, it matters little what places they take.

To Resist Cavalry.

When the square is to prepare for cavalry, upon the word READY, the first and second rank will sink down at once upon the right knee, as a front and rear rank kneeling, in the manner prescribed when at the capping position, and at the same time they will place the butts of their rifles on the ground against the inside of their right knees, locks turned uppermost, the

**PREPARE FOR
CAVALRY,
READY.** muzzle slanting upwards, so that the point of the sword will be about the height of a horse's nose ; the left hand to have a firm grasp of the rifle immediately above the lower band, the right hand holding the small of the butt, the left arm to rest upon the thigh about six inches in rear of the left knee. The third and fourth ranks will make ready as a front and rear rank standing. Muzzles of rifles to be inclined upwards. The standing ranks will fire by files, and the kneeling ranks in volleys by word of command.

When the sides of the square are less than four deep, the front rank only will kneel.

In this manner dispersed parties may be formed to resist an attack of cavalry in an open country, either in one or more squares, according as they may be more or less dispersed ; each square consisting of any number of men. Every man will run to the nearest rallying point, but the larger the square the safer it will be.

**RE-FORM
SQUAD.** When the square is to be re-formed into a squad in line, the right or left hand man will be placed facing the supposed enemy, and the remainder of the men will form upon him.

SIXTH LESSON.

Formation of the Corps or Company.

The corps will fall in in two ranks in the same manner as the squads have been taught.

It will then number off from right to left, and will be divided into two subdivisions; and four sections, as nearly as possible of equal strength.

When one subdivision has a file more than the other, it will be the right subdivision; if one section has a file more than the rest, it will be the first or right section ; when two sections have a file more each than the other two, they will be the first and fourth, that is, the right and left sections. If three sections have a file each more than

PLATE III.

Fig. 1.
FORMATION OF A COMPANY OR CORPS.

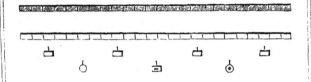

Fig. 2.
BY SECTIONS RIGHT WHEEL—QUICK-MARCH.

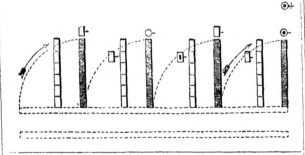

Fig. 3.
FORM CLOSE COLUMN OF SECTIONS—QUICK-MARCH.

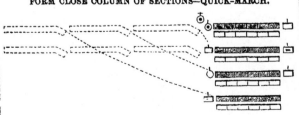

the remaining section, the first, second, and fourth will have the extra files, the third being the weakest, thus :—

	Left Subdivision.		Right Subdivision.	
—	4th Section.	3rd Section.	2nd Section.	1st Section.
A Company of 17 Files	17, 16, 15, 14	13, 12, 11, 10	9, 8, 7, 6	5, 4, 3, 2, 1
,, 18 ,,	18, 17, 16, 15, 14	13, 12, 11, 10	9, 8, 7, 6	5, 4, 3, 2, 1
,, 19 ,,	19, 18, 17, 16, 15	14, 13, 12, 11	10, 9, 8, 7, 6	5, 4, 3, 2, 1
,, 20 ,,	20, 19, 18, 17, 16	15, 14, 13, 12, 11	10, 9, 8, 7, 6	5, 4, 3, 2, 1

Posts of Officers.—Plate III., fig. 1.

The post of the captain is in front of the centre of his corps, at about three paces distance, except when it is extended in skirmishing order, or when it has to fire, in which cases he will be in rear of the centre.

The lieutenant will take charge of the right subdivision; the ensign of the left; and they will be posted respectively at two paces distance in rear of the centre files of their subdivisions. One non-commissioned officer will be attached to each section; he will take post one pace in rear of the centre of his section: and one non-commissioned officer, called the covering serjeant, will be attached to the captain to take up points for him or assist him in any manner; he will be posted two paces in rear of the centre of the company, ready to run out, when required, on either flank.

If the corps is ordered to march by the right, the lieutenant will move up to the right of the front rank, and lead; if it is ordered to march by the left, the ensign will move up to the left of the front rank, and lead. The flank which directs is called the pivot flank, the opposite flank the reserve flank. The officer, or non-commissioned officer, on the flank of a company, subdivision, or section, is called its leader.

Dispersing and Assembling.

Men after being told off should be wheeled into column of sections, and their leaders placed in front of them, so that they may know each other, and during a drill the corps should frequently be dispersed and then ordered to close again, on which the men will run in and form on their section leaders, who will stand in a row one behind the other, to mark the left of their respective sections in regular order, at section distance from each other. This will be found a most useful practice.

Advancing, Retiring, Wheeling, &c.

The company or corps will be practised in advancing and retiring in line, in wheeling to the right and left, and in dressing, in the same manner as they have been taught in the squad drill.

Wheeling into Column of Subdivisions or Sections.
Plate III., fig. 2.

BY
SUBDIVISIONS
(or SECTIONS)
RIGHT (or
LEFT) WHEEL,
QUICK–MARCH,
FORWARD.

Volunteers will also be taught to wheel to the right or left by subdivisions or sections, each subdivision, or section, wheeling in the same manner as a squad, and when square, on the word FORWARD, they will move on in column; when in subdivisions the lieutenant and ensign will lead their respective subdivisions, when in sections the lieutenant and ensign will take the leading sections of their respective subdivision, the two remaining sections will be led by their respective non-commissioned officer. When taking ground to the right, that is right subdivision or section in front, the leaders will be on the left of the front rank of their respective subdivision or section ; when taking ground to the left, that is left subdivision or section in front, the leaders will be on the right of their front ranks. In these formations the captain will place himself about two paces from the pivot flank of the leading subdivision or section.

The corps will also be practised together in the rifle exercise already taught.

They will next be taught to form company square in the following manner.

Company Square.—Plate III., fig. 3.

FORM CLOSE
COLUMN OF–
SECTIONS.

On the word SECTIONS, the first section will fix swords and the rear rank will take a pace of 24 inches to the front ; the second, third, and fourth sections will face to the right, their leading files disengaging to the rear.

QUICK-MARCH. On the word MARCH, the sections which have faced, will step off and form close column in rear of the right section, the rear ranks closing on the front ranks during the march; each section will halt front and fix swords without word of command as it arrives in column; the distance between sections will be one pace.

PREPARE FOR CAVALRY. On the word PREPARE FOR CAVALRY, the officers and non-commissioned officers will move into the centre of the column; the men will then face outwards, so as to show a front of equal strength in every direction.

READY. On the word READY, the men will proceed as directed in the rallying square.

The company will be re-formed as follows :—

RE-FORM—COLUMN. On the word COLUMN, the men will face to their proper front in column, the captain and supernumeraries* will move out to their places on the flanks.

RE-FORM—COMPANY. On the word COMPANY, the second, third, and fourth sections will face to the left.

QUICK-MARCH. On the word MARCH, they will move out, each section turning to its front when clear, and dressing up into line with the first section without word of command, the rear rank resuming its proper distance.

If the men count the number of paces that take them into column, by taking the same number when re-forming company, they will be able to turn to the front together. The swords will be unfixed by word of command.

A close column of subdivisions will be formed in the same manner as a close column of sections.

Skirmishing.

The company must also be practised in extending and closing from the halt and on the march, advancing and retiring, inclining to the right and left, and changing front, as already taught.

---

* Subaltern officers, except when they are in command of the company, and the serjeants, are called supernumeraries.

The volunteers should also be taught to form close column of sections from extended order on any section ; when on a centre or left section, those from the right will form in front of it in regular order. They should also be practised in forming rallying square or squares, as already taught.

One subdivision should also be taught to extend while the other remains at 150 or 200 paces in rear of its centre to support it ; when two companies are moving together, one will support the other.

Skirmishers closing on the Support.—Plate IV.

1. *Calling in Skirmishers.* Fig. 1.—When the skirmishers are called in to their support, the two centre files will retire in quick time, opening out as they move to the rear to clear the front of the support ; the remaining files will close upon them in double time on the march ; when at quarter distance in rear of the support they will turn inwards, shouldering arms as they turn ; and when they meet in rear of the centre of the support they will halt front, order arms, and stand at ease.

2. *Closing for Cavalry.* Fig. 2.—If cavalry approaches, the support will immediately advance, and as the skirmishers approach, it will halt, and if consisting of a subdivision, will double one section close behind the other ; if consisting of a company, it will double one subdivision in rear of the other ; the skirmishers will run in in rear of the support, keeping well clear of its front, and will cluster close together, forming the rear of the square like a rallying square. If the skirmishers cannot reach their support, they can always form rallying square, and the support will then form a rallying square, or a square in close column of sections, according to its strength.

Relieving Skirmishers.

When skirmishers have suffered considerable loss, when they are fatigued by continued rapid movements, or when their supply of ammunition is getting low, it will be advisable to relieve them.

The most convenient method of effecting the relief is to order the support to extend and relieve its skirmishers.

When retiring, the successive relief of the skirmishers by supports, is the most effectual manner of keeping an enemy

PLATE IV.

Fig. 1.

SKIRMISHERS CLOSING ON THEIR SUPPORT.

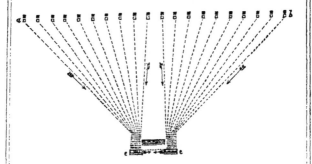

Fig. 2.

CLOSING ON SUPPORT IN PRESENCE OF CAVALRY.

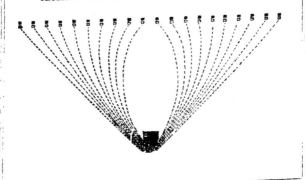

C

in check. The officer commanding a support should therefore be constantly on the look-out for good positions, in which he may extend his men with advantage, such as a bank, a ditch, a wall, or such like cover. After relieving, the new skirmishers must hold their position until ordered to continue the retreat.

The following general rules are laid down for relieving skirmishers under different circumstances :—

1. *Relieving Skirmishers that are halted.*—To relieve skirmishers that are halted, the support will extend in the rear, out of immediate reach of the enemy's fire, and then run up to the old line. The old skirmishers on being relieved, will run straight to their rear, and when out of immediate reach of the enemy's fire, will close on the centre and form support.

Should an immediate advance be intended, the old skirmishers, on being relieved, will remain lying down till the new skirmishers have gained sufficient distance to their front; they will then rise, close on the centre, and form support.

2. *Relieving Skirmishers that are advancing.*—The support will extend on the march and then double up to the old skirmishers, changing into quick time as it passes through them, on which the old line will lie down and wait till the new skirmishers are sufficiently advanced to protect them from immediate fire, when they will rise and close to the centre, forming the support.

3. *Relieving Skirmishers that are retiring.*—To relieve skirmishers that are retiring, the support will halt, and front, at a considerable distance in the rear, and will then extend, each man, if possible, getting under cover. When the old skirmishers arrive within about twenty or thirty paces of the new, they will run through them to the rear until they are out of immediate reach of the enemy's fire, and then close on the centre and form support.

Bugle Calls.

The following bugle sounds may occasionally be substituted for words of command when skirmishing, but the voice is less liable to error, and commands can be passed down an extended line with great rapidity by the supernumeraries :—

One G sounded on the bugle denotes the right of the line ; two G's the centre ; three G's the left.

c 2

The G's, preceding any sound, denote the part of the line to which it applies; for instance, two G's before the extend signify to extend from the centre; one G followed by the close, to close to the right; one G followed by the incline, to incline to the right; three G's followed by the wheel, to wheel to the left.

I. Extend.

II. Close.

III. Advance.

IV. Halt.

The Halt annuls all previous Sounds except the Fire.

V. Commence Firing.

VI. Cease Firing.

VII. Retire.

VIII. Assembly.

This sound will be used to turn out troops in cases of alarm by day or night, but must not be used at light infantry drill.

IX. Incline.

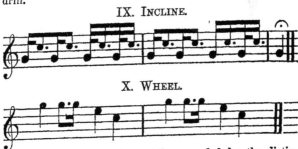

X. Wheel.

The calls IX. and X. must be preceded by the distinguishing G's.

XI. The Alarm or Look out for Cavalry.

ADDITIONAL INSTRUCTION.

The foregoing lessons contain all the drill volunteers need know ; but if they have time to learn more, the formation of four deep will be found useful.

A corps taking ground to a flank by fours will be led by the subaltern of the leading subdivision, who will place himself on that flank of the leading four which is composed of the front-rank men ; the other subaltern and the serjeants will remain on the reverse flanks of the files they cover when in line. The same rule applies to file marching.

The Formation of Fours.

SQUAD, FOURS—DEEP.	On the word DEEP, the left files will double behind the right files by taking a pace to the rear with their left feet, and a pace to the right with their right feet.
SQUAD-FRONT.	On the word FRONT, the left files will move up in line with the right files, by taking a pace to the left with their left feet, and a pace to the front with their right feet.
SQUAD, FOURS—ABOUT.	On the word ABOUT, the squad will form fours deep as above described, and then face to the right about.
SQUAD—FRONT.	On the word FRONT, the whole squad will face to the right about and re-form two deep, as already described.
SQUAD, FOURS—RIGHT.	On the word RIGHT, the squad will face to the right, and the left files will form on the right of the right files, by taking one pace to the right with their right feet, and one pace to the front with their left feet.
SQUAD—FRONT.	On the word FRONT, the squad will face to the left and re-form two deep, as already described.
SQUAD, FOURS—LEFT.	On the word LEFT, the squad will face to the left, and the left files will form on the left of the right files, by taking one pace to the left with their left feet and one pace to the rear with their right feet.
SQUAD-FRONT.	On the word FRONT, the squad will face to the right and re-form two deep, as already described.

Corps or Companies moving together as a Battalion.

Although rifle volunteers may in some instances be organized in battalions, and independent corps may occasionally meet and move together, it is not necessary that they should learn complicated battalion evolutions.

The following formations and movements are all that can be required, and as they are simply combinations of the company movements already explained in this manual, it is only necessary for the officers to study their details.

Formation of Open Column.

In open column the companies will be formed one behind another, each at a distance equal to its own front from the company that is next before it, measuring from the heels of the front rank men of one company to the heels of the front rank men of the other ; this is also called wheeling distance.*

The captains will take post on the pivot flanks of their respective front ranks, covering correctly one behind another, the men touching in to them.

The covering serjeants will be in rear of their captains on the pivot flank of the rear rank, the remaining serjeants and the subaltern officers will remain in their usual places in rear of the companies.

When a column is on the march the captains must be careful to preserve their proper distances; but they must not attempt to preserve their covering in one straight line from the front to the rear of the column, unless they are marching on an alignment, each captain should follow the footsteps of the captain next in front of him.

Telling off the Battalion.

When the battalion is formed the commanding officer will give the command, TELL OFF THE BATTALION, on which the captains will take a pace to their front, face towards their men, the captain of the leading company will call out No. 1, the captain of the second company will then call out No. 2, and so on to the rear ; when all are numbered, the commanding officer will give the command EYES-FRONT, on which the captains will resume their posts.

---

* Covering serjeants, in taking up wheeling distance for their companies, may remember that by multiplying the number of files by 7, and dividing the product by 10, they will get the required number of paces.

Pivot Flank.

The above formation of open column is called "right in "front," because the company (No. 1) which is on the right, when in line, is in front. When No. 1 company is in rear, and the highest numbered company in front, the column is called left in front. In the former case the left of each company will be the pivot flank, in the latter the right.

Formation of Quarter Distance Column.

The formation of a quarter distance column is the same as that of an open column, except that the companies are at a distance equal only to the front of one section (quarter of a company) from each other.

Formation of Line.

When the companies of a battalion are formed in line there will be no interval between them, they will be placed in regular order, No. 1 on the right, the highest number on the left. The captains will be on the right of the front ranks of their respective companies, the covering serjeants behind them on the right of the rear ranks ; in other respects the companies will be formed as usual.

When a line is ordered to advance it will move by the centre, the captain who happens to be in the centre must therefore be careful in selecting his points to march upon, as he will direct the line.

Post of Captain in Subdivisions, Sections, or Fours.

When a company, in battalion drill, moves by subdivisions, sections, or fours, the captain will lead, in place of the subaltern, by the left or right according as right or left is in front. The subaltern of the leading subdivision, when in column of subdivisions, will follow in rear of the centre of his subdivision; when in column of sections he will lead the second section; when in fours he will march on the reverse flank of the centre four of his subdivision.

Telling off afresh.

When companies lose their relative position in line or column, which may frequently be the case after skirmishing they can tell off afresh.

Movements.

The details of the following movements, as far as they are applicable to the volunteer drill, may be learned by the officers from the " FIELD EXERCISE AND EVOLUTIONS OF " INFANTRY."

1. *Wheeling into Line from Open Column, F.E., Part III., Section 2.*
2. *Wheeling into Open Column from Line, F. E., Part III., Sections 26 and 27.*
3. *A Battalion in Line forming Open or Quarter Distance Column, F.E., Part III., Section 32.*
4. *A Battalion in Quarter Distance Column deploying into Line, F.E., Part III., Sections 38, 39, and 40.*
5. *A Column at Quarter Distance wheeling on a moveable Pivot, F.E., Part III., Section 16.*
6. *An Open Column closing to Quarter Distance, F.E., Part III., Section 12.*
7. *A Quarter Distance Column opening out to Company Distance (Open Column), F.E., Part III., Section 13.*

Squares.

The simplest method of forming square to resist cavalry when in column, is to close to the front on the leading company, the rear ranks also closing on the front ranks, then face outwards and prepare for cavalry, as in rallying square. When in line, wheel into column, and proceed as above described.

Corps that have time to learn the formation of a more complicated square, are recommended to practise the light infantry square, explained in Part IV., Section 16, of the " Field Exercise," as it is applicable to any number of companies, from two upwards.

Skirmishing.

A battalion may send out any number of companies to skirmish, according to its strength, and the extent of ground that is to be covered ; each company that is sent out to skirmish must have a company in support, as a general rule about 200 yards in rear of its centre ; the reserve should always be composed of at least one-third of

c 5

the whole battalion ; it will be placed at about 500 yards in rear of the centre of the skirmishers.

When a line of skirmishers composed of several companies advances or retires, it will move by the centre of the whole line, except while inclining to a flank, when it will move by the flank to which it is inclining.

A line of skirmishers composed of several companies will change front as described in the sixth lesson of this manual, the supports following the movements of the skirmishers.

The directions already given for the movements of the skirmishers and supports in case of the approach of cavalry, are equally applicable to the companies of a battalion ; the reserve will advance on the first alarm, and form square when necessary ; the captains must as far as possible form their squares so as to flank each other.

When required to assemble, the skirmishers will at all times form first on their supports, after which they may both be brought in, and formed at quarter distance in rear of the reserve.

Inspection.

When a corps of rifle volunteers is inspected, it will be formed in line in the usual manner, and will present arms on the approach of the inspecting officer, the commanding officer of the corps or battalion saluting with his sword.

Should the corps be required to march past, it will move at quick time, as described in the F.E., Part VI., Section 1, "*Marching Past in Quick Time.*"

If the corps consists of one company, the captain will march in his usual place, in front ; if it consists of several companies, the captains will march on the flanks of the companies, proceeding as explained in the above-named section.

The commanding officer of the corps only, whether mounted or on foot, will salute with his sword as he approaches within ten paces of the inspecting officer.

Formation of an Advanced Guard on a Road.—
Plate V.

16. *Formation of an Advanced Guard on a Road.—* When a column is marching along a road, the advanced guard will be composed of one or more companies, divided into four parts or sections ; the two rear sections (under

PLATE V.

the command of the senior officer) will form the reserve in front of the column ; the second section from the front will form a support 200 yards in front of the reserve, under command of the third senior officer ; the leading section will be 100 yards in front of the second section, and will detach a corporal and two files 100 yards to its front and two files to each flank, 100 yards from the road and about 50 yards more retired than the corporal's party. The senior subaltern will accompany the leading section. The detached files must carefully examine all houses, enclosures, &c. within their reach ; but should more distant objects present themselves, patroles must be detached from the second section for their particular examination. Single files of communication will be placed between the different divisions of an advanced guard, and also between its reserve and the head of the column. The distance between the two latter must be regulated by circumstances ; but it will generally be about 500 yards during the day and about 300 during the night.

If the company is weak, it may be advisable to send on only one file and a corporal in front, and one file on each flank.

In open country an advanced guard is simply a line of skirmishers, with a support, and, if necessary, a reserve.

Marching at Ease.

Volunteers should not be required to march long distances at attention ; they should be ordered to MARCH AT EASE, on which they may carry their rifles in any manner they please, and loosen out their files to the reverse flank ; but they must take care not to hang back, and open out to the rear, nor lose their places, lest they retard other corps that may be following them. On the word ATTENTION, they will close in again to the pivot flank, and trail arms properly in the right hand.

INSTRUCTION OF MUSKETRY.

CLEANING ARMS.

Every volunteer must learn the names of the different parts of his rifle, and the way to clean it, and keep it in order.

NAMES OF THE DIFFERENT PARTS OF THE RIFLE.

PLATE VI.

Fig. 1. STOCK.	Fig. 2. BARREL AND RAMROD.
A. nose cap.	A. muzzle.
B. upper band.	B. front or foresight.
C. lower band.	D. flanges.
D. swell.	C. back or elevating sight. E. flap.
E, E. projections.	F. slider.
F. head.	G. spring.
G. small.	H. bed.
H. trigger guard.	K. nipple lump.
K. trigger plate.	L. nipple.
L. trigger.	M. breech.
M. breech nail.	N. breech pin.
N, N. side nails.	O. breech nail hole.
	T. catch.
O. butt. P. toe. Q. heel.	P, P. ramrod.
	Q. head.
R. heel plate.	R. point.
S, S. sling.	S. shaft.
T, V. upper and lower swivels.	
W. snap cap.	

The side of the rifle on which the lock is placed is called the lock side.

Fig. 3. SWORD AND SCABBARD.

A. blade. B. hilt. C. guard and ring. D. spring. E. scabbard.

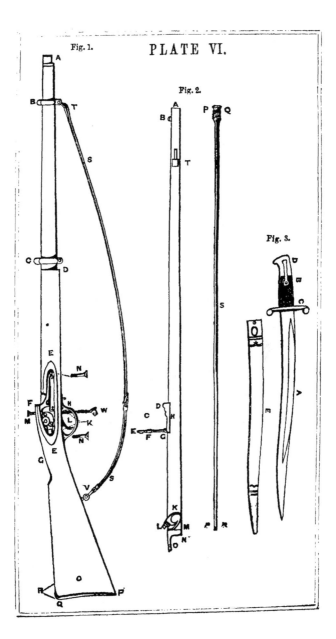

Fig. 1.

PLATE VI.

Fig. 2.

Fig. 3.

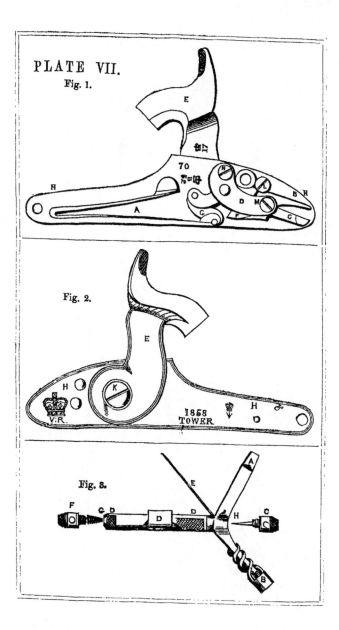

PLATE VII.

Fig. 1.

Fig. 2.

Fig. 3.

Plate VII.

Fig. 1 and 2.—Lock.

A. main-spring.	G. swivel.
B. sear-spring.	H, H. lock plate.
C. sear.	K. tumbler nail or pin.
D. bridle.	L. sear-spring nail.
E. hammer.	M. sear nail.
F. tumbler.	N. bridle nail.

Fig. 3.—Nipple Wrench, &c.

A. turn screw.	E. picker.
B. worm.	F. ball drawer.
C. drift.	G. nipple wrench.
D, D, D. cramp.	H. oil bottle.

Cleaning the Barrel.

1. Place the rifle at full cock, and draw the ramrod.

2. Put a piece of rag, woollen if possible, or tow, into the jag, and twist it round so as to cover it.

3. Hold the rifle in the left hand, at the full extent of the arm, barrel downwards, with the forefinger and thumb in line with, and round the muzzle, heel of the butt resting on the ground to the rear.

4. Pour about a quarter of a pint of water into the barrel with care, so as to prevent any of it getting between stock and barrel, or into the lock through the tumbler axle hole ; immediately afterwards put the ramrod into the barrel, and sponge or rub it carefully up and down to remove the dirt or fouling, forcing the water through the nipple to clear the touch-hole. Repeat this process until the barrel is quite clean.

5. Wipe the barrel well out with rag or tow until it is perfectly dry, and afterwards with an oiled rag ; then put the muzzle stopper in the barrel, and the snap cap on the nipple. Care should be taken to keep the snap cap dry when washing out the barrel, and to wipe the mouth of the hammer before letting it down on the snap cap.

6. On the following morning, and on every occasion before using the rifle, wipe the barrel out perfectly clean and dry.

7. The fouling which settles on the stock near the nipple lump when firing should, if possible, be removed without using water or a damp rag. On no account is a knife or sharp instrument of any description to be used to remove the dirt near the nipple lump or trigger plate.

8. By the foregoing mode of cleaning, the liability of the barrel to become rusty will be very much reduced, and the frequent necessity for removing it from the stock, which is always objectionable, be obviated.

9. In order to prevent water soaking into the stock, and at the same time to give it a smooth and polished appearance, rub it over well with oil, and apply a little bees-wax between it and the barrel, and between the lock plate and stock, to prevent water getting under the barrel or into the lock.

Dismounting the Lock.

1st. Unscrew and remove the tumbler pin.
2d. Put the lock at full cock, then place the cramp on the mainspring, and, after letting the hammer down, remove it.
3d. Partly unscrew the sear-spring pin, then place the edge of the turnscrew between the bend of the sear-spring and lock-plate, to raise the former from the latter, after which unscrew the sear-spring pin, and remove the sear-spring.
4th. Unscrew the sear-pin and remove sear.
5th. Unscrew the bridle-pin and remove bridle.
6th. Remove the hammer (which is to rest in the hollow of the hand) by a few smart taps,—as near the lock-plate as possible,—with something softer than itself.
7th. Remove the tumbler.
8th. Remove the swivel from the tumbler.

Cleaning the Lock.

1. When the lock is dismounted, wipe the several limbs, first with an oiled rag, and afterwards with a rag quite dry.

2. If any specks of rust are seen, either on the lock (more particularly the tumbler axle hole) or any of the limbs, they are to be removed with an oiled rag. No brick-dust, or powder of any kind, is to be used for this purpose, as such would have the effect of removing the case hardening from those parts that are not steel, and thus render them much more liable to rust.

3. In remounting the lock the threads of the several pins, as also the pivot and axle of tumbler, and pivots of swivel,

should be oiled before putting them in their respective places, in order that they may work easily.

4. The other frictional parts of the lock to which it is essential to apply oil (which should be animal and not vegetable) are the nose of the sear, and between the sear and sear spring. Only a very small quantity of oil should be used, and applied either with a feather or the point of the pricker, as too much is likely to clog the parts.

Remounting the Lock.

1. Attach the swivel to the tumbler.
2. Place the tumbler in the lock-plate.
3. Fix the bridle on the pivot of the tumbler, and its stud in the lock-plate; then screw home the bridle-pin, which differs from the other pins (which are rounded off) by being flat at the end.
4. Place the sear between the bridle and the lock-plate, with its nose against the tumbler, and screw home the sear-pin.
5. Partly screw the sear-spring to the lock-plate, then with the thumb of the left hand press the spring against the body of the sear until the stud enters the stud-hole, and screw home the sear-spring pin.
6. Fix the hammer on the squares of the tumbler in a position as if on the nipple, and screw home the tumbler-pin.
7. Attach the swivel by its pivots to the claws of the mainspring, then put on the mainspring, by placing the stud in the lock-plate, and its catch against the fore-stud; after which place the lock at full-cock to remove the cramp; this being done, ease the lock to half-cock.

Theoretical Principles.

Every volunteer should understand the reasons for the rules, which are laid down for his guidance in practice. The following explanations will be found sufficient, though, where musketry instructors are employed, and time will permit, they may be given more at length.

1. The axis of the piece is an imaginary line along the centre of the barrel A, B, fig. 1, Plate VIII.

2. The "line of fire" (B, C) is the continuation of the axis, and the direction in which the bullet would fly, with uniform velocity, were it not impeded by the resistance of the atmosphere and drawn down by the force of gravity.

3. The air is an elastic fluid that resists the bullet and reduces its velocity ; the greater the velocity with which the bullet proceeds, the greater is the resistance it meets.

The "force of gravity" draws the bullet downwards from the moment it quits the muzzle, and acts with increased power the longer the bullet is exposed to its influence. These two powers combined, the one increasing as the other diminishes, cause the bullet to fly in a curved line, called the trajectory, B, D, fig. 1, Plate VIII.

According to the above principles, if the axis of the rifle were directed to an object C, fig. 1, Plate VIII., in a target, when fired, the bullet could not hit that mark, as the air and force of gravity would oblige it to fly along the trajectory to the point D, which would actually in the first 100 yards, be 1 foot 5 inches lower down ; therefore, in order to hit the point C, it is necessary to elevate the muzzle till the axis of the barrel is directed to a point E, 1 foot 5 inches above it. To enable this to be done, the sights K, L, fig. 2, are so arranged as to place the rifle, when they are both accurately brought up to the line of sight, which is the line F, C, between the eye and the point aimed at, exactly in the required position.

If, however, the target were removed to a greater distance, and the rifle were fired from the same position, the bullet would follow the trajectory, and strike a point H below the point G aimed at ; it is necessary, therefore, to increase the elevation of the muzzle as the distance increases, for which purpose the back sight is furnished with a flap and slider marked with the distances up to 1100 yards for which the elevations are required.

The thickness of the barrel at the breech is greater than its thickness at the muzzle, which in itself gives elevation ; combined with this the lowest sight is arranged to give the proper elevation for 100 yards ; when firing at a shorter distance it is therefore necessary to fire a little under the mark, at 50 yards about 8 inches, at 30 yards about 4 inches.

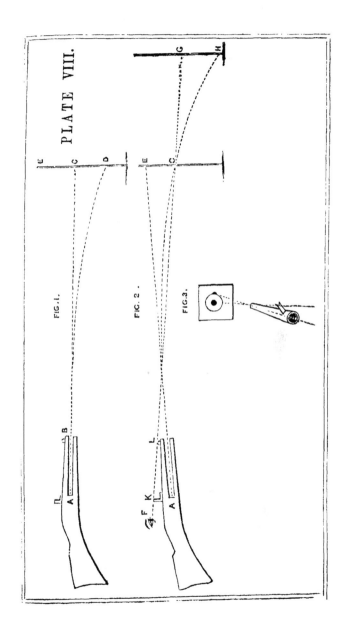

PLATE VIII.

FIG. 1.

FIG. 2.

FIG. 3.

The volunteer must be very careful that he holds the sight of his rifle quite upright when taking aim; if it inclines to either side, instead of hitting the mark aimed at, the ball will invariably strike on that side to which the sight is inclined. See fig. 3, Plate VIII.

Allowance must be made for the wind, when firing, but the extent of the allowance can only be learned by experience.

If in loading the volunteer observes that there is not sufficient powder in the cartridge, or should he accidentally spill any, he must in firing aim a little high, otherwise the bullet will fall short of the mark.

Aiming Drill.

1. A musketry instructor or an experienced shot must superintend each squad, at this and the following drills; the squad should not exceed ten men.

2. In this exercise the volunteer is to be instructed how to aim and to adjust the back-sight of his rifle, and his progress is to be tested by making him aim at the different distances by means of a rest. If traversing rests are not available, a tripod formed of three stakes tied or looped near the top, supporting a bag of sand about $4\frac{1}{2}$ feet from the ground, will answer the purpose.

3. The instructor is first to explain the principles of aligning the sights of the rifle on an object, confining the attention of the volunteer to the following simple rules:—

    1st. That the sights should not incline to the right or left.

    2nd. That the line of sight should be taken along the centre of the notch of the back-sight and the top of the fore-sight, which should cover the middle of the mark aimed at.

    3rd. That the eye should be fixed stedfastly on the mark aimed at, and not on the barrel or fore-sight; the sights will then be brought up to the line of sight.

    4th. That in aiming the left eye should be closed. If a man is not able to do this at the outset, he will soon succeed by tying a handkerchief over the left eye.

4. The instructor will also explain the difference between fine, full, and half sight in aiming, as follows, viz. :—

1st. Fine-sight is when the line of sight is taken along

Fig. 1.   A   the bottom of the notch of the back-sight, the fine point of the fore-sight being only seen in the alignment ; as A, fig. 1.

2nd. Full-sight is when the point of the fore-sight

Fig. 2.   B   is taken in alignment with the shoulder of the notch of the back-sight ; as B, fig. 2.

3rd. Half-sight is when the point of the fore-sight is

Fig. 3.   C   aligned midway between the shoulder and bottom of back-sight ; as C, fig. 3.

5. Aiming with the half-sight is the usual method ; aiming with a fine-sight will give a little less elevation ; and aiming with a full-sight a little more.

6. The instructor will next cause each man to place his rifle in the rest and align it with the sight for 100 yards on a mark that distance from him ; having done so, he will leave his rifle on the rest and step aside. The instructor will then see if the aim is correct, and should he discover any error, he will point it out and cause it to be corrected, or call upon another volunteer to correct it.

7. The foregoing proceeding is to be carried out, at every distance of 50 yards, from 100 to 900 yards, at " bulls' eyes " of the following dimensions, viz. :—

From 100 to 300 yards, eight inches in diameter.
From 350 to 900 yards, two feet.

Position Drill.

In this drill the volunteers will be put through the following practices in squads of about ten men each, formed in single rank, at one pace apart, great care being taken that all their positions and movements are correct. When coming to the "present," they should be taught to aim at small "bulls' eyes," painted as described in the Platoon Exercise, page 23.

First Practice.

In the first practice after the caution, POSITION DRILL, FIRST PRACTICE AS A FRONT (or REAR) RANK, STANDING (or KNEELING), the word AT—YARDS—READY will be given, on which the volunteer will proceed as described in the Platoon Exercise. On the word PRESENT, without moving the body, head, or eye, the volunteer will throw the rifle smartly to the front of the right shoulder to the full extent of the left arm (the arms moving close in to the body) ; he will raise the rifle in so doing, keeping the sight upright ; the top part of the heel plate to be in a line with the top of the shoulder, the muzzle to be a few inches below the mark the eyes are fixed upon, the forefinger to be extended along the outside of the trigger guard, and both elbows to be inclined downwards. On the word TWO, he will bring the rifle smartly to the hollow of the right shoulder, as described in the Platoon Exercise. On the word THREE, he will bring the rifle down to the capping position without altering the position of the body, head, or eye ; in this manner the motions of the "Present" must be repeated several times, after which, on the word EASE SPRINGS, the volunteer will let the hammer down on the nipple, and will be directed to ORDER ARMS and STAND AT EASE.

After this, the volunteer will go through the practice, judging his own time, on the words AT—YARDS READY, FIRST PRACTICE JUDGING YOUR OWN TIME — PRESENT. When he has repeated the motions several times, without further word of command, on the word STEADY he will cease the practice, remaining at the capping position till directed to EASE SPRINGS—ORDER—ARMS and STAND AT EASE.

Second Practice.

In the second practice, the volunteer will go through all the motions of the "Ready" and "Present" by numbers, as explained in the Platoon Exercise, except that on the word FIVE, he will bring his rifle down to the capping position, and full cock, after which the movements of the "Present" will be repeated several times.

Third Practice.

In the third practice the volunteer will go through the motions of loading, standing, and judging his own time ; he will then practise independent file firing both standing and kneeling.

Snapping Caps and Blank Firing.

Volunteers who have not been accustomed to firing should first be practised in snapping caps while taking aim, until the tendency to wink at the explosion is overcome, after which they should be practised in firing blank cartridge to accustom them to the recoil of the rifle. About 10 caps fired at different drills should suffice for the former practice, with 10 rounds of blank cartridge for the latter; 5 caps or rounds to be fired singly, 2 by file, and 3 in volleys.

Judging Distance Drill.

As proper elevation is of such great importance in firing, the volunteer should be well practised in judging distances ; for this purpose men should be placed in front of the squad, at measured distances of 50 yards apart, from 50 to 300 yards for the first practice, and afterwards from 300 to 900 yards. The attention of each volunteer should be directed to the appearance of these men, and of their features, accoutrements, &c., at the different distances ; they must remember the distances at which the smaller objects become indistinct or invisible. Each volunteer should be called upon to explain to the instructor what he sees ; the explanation should be in a low tone of voice, in order that the rest of the squad may not hear.

It must be explained to the volunteer that the sun, the state of the atmosphere, and the background will make a difference in the appearance of the same objects at different times.

After the above exercises, volunteers should be practised in judging unknown distances; the accuracy of their judgment will be tested, by measuring the distances with a chain or cord.

Target Practice.

1. The volunteer having been thoroughly practised in the foregoing exercises, he will go through a course of target practice.

2. The targets are to be six feet in height and two in breadth, constructed of iron of sufficient thickness to be rifle bullet proof ; they should be coloured white with a mixture of whiting and size ; the bull's eye and circle describing the "centre," black, with lamp-black, water, and size.

PLATE IX.

MARKERS BUTT.

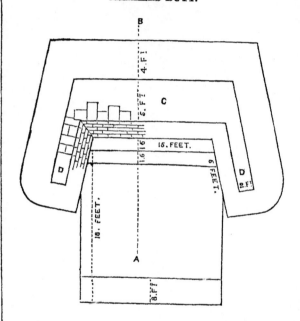

This is the smallest description of Butt that ought ever to be made, and the markers must always sit on the upper banquette close to the interior slope, which is to be revetted with turf.

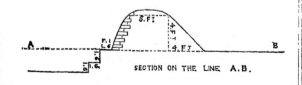

SECTION ON THE LINE A.B.

3. Great care must be taken in lowering or raising the targets to prevent them being damaged.

4. In all cases where the nature of the ground admits of it, a trench is to be dug for the "markers," of the dimensions given in Plate IX., about fifteen yards to the front, and to one side of the targets, and in such a position that the markers may easily see the face of the target from it ; the earth excavated should be thrown up on the side of the firing C ; there should also be two epaulments, D, D, so as to screen the men not only from the shots themselves, but from any stones that may be thrown up by them.

5. The shots that strike the target are to be denoted by flags* of different colours raised above the butt. These flags, together with the number of points fixed as the value of the shots, are as follows :—

	Shots.	Flags.	Value in points.
In the practices to 300 yards inclusive.	Outer	- White or yellow	- 1
	Centre	- Dark blue	- 2
	Bull's-eye	- Red and white	- 3
	Ricochet	- Red flag waved in front of the butt R	
	Miss	- - -	- 0
In the practices at distances beyond 300 yards.	Outer	- White or yellow -	- 1
	Centre	- Dark blue -	- 2
	Ricochet	- Red flag waved in front of the butt R	
	Miss	- -	- 0

6. Ricochets, or shots which strike the ground before hitting the target, are to be signalled by waving the red flag twice to and fro in front of the target, and are to be counted as misses in individual firing, but noted in the register by the letter R.

7. The signal for "danger," or "cease firing," is in all cases to be a red flag, which will be hoisted and planted on the top of the butt, whenever it is necessary to cease firing to re-colour the targets, or for any other purpose.

8. Whenever a shot strikes to the right, the flag denoting its value is to be inclined to the right, and *vice versâ.*

---

* The number of flags required is as follows, viz.:—

1 Large red flag, 6 feet square, to be planted in a conspicuous place in the neighbourhood of the range before the firing commences, and to remain till it is over, to warn persons off the ground.

4 { 2 red	do. 2½	„	for the use of look-out men.
{ 2 { do.	do.	one for use at the firing point.
{ do.	do.	
1 red and white do.	do.	
1 dark blue do.	do.	for use in the marker's butt.
1 white do.	do.	

The large flag may be obtained for 3s., and the smaller ones for 1s. 8d. ; lance poles 10 feet long should not cost more than 2s. 4d.

When the shot strikes high, the flag is to be raised as high as possible, and when low, it is only to be raised high enough to be easily visible above the butt.

9. The section or squad is always to load by word of command. When everything is ready to commence, a signal will be made to the markers, and as soon as the danger flag is lowered, the officer is to order the practice to go on. The right-hand man of the front rank will then take a pace to his front, come to the capping position, and fire ; after which he will come to the shoulder from the capping position, and form three paces to the rear of the point he previously occupied ; the next man of the front rank will then move to the front and fire.

10. Whenever the hits on the target become too numerous to distinguish quite easily the new ones as they strike, the target is to be coloured afresh.

11. Every volunteer is to expend in his course of practice 90 rounds of ball ammunition, in the following manner, viz. :—

> 60 in individual firing,
> 10 by files,
> 10 in volleys, and
> 10 in skirmishing order.

12. The number of rounds to be expended at each distance, the distances and number of targets to be fired at by the several classes in individual firing, and the size of the bull's-eye, and centre for each class, are as follows :—

	Yards.		Rounds.		
3rd class.	150 -	-	- 5	Two targets placed together.	Having a bull's-eye eight inches in diameter, and a black circle two feet in diameter.
	200 -	-	- 5		
	250 -	-	- 5		
	300 -	-	- 5		
2nd class.	400 -	-	- 5	Four targets placed together.	Having a black centre two feet in diameter and no circle.
	500 -	-	- 5		
	550 -	-	- 5		
	600 -	-	- 5		
1st class.	650 -	-	- 5	Six targets placed together.	Having a black centre three feet in diameter and no circle.
	700 -	-	- 5		
	800 -	-	- 5		
	900 -	-	- 5		

13. Volunteers should never fire more than 10 rounds at any one practice.

File Firing and Volley Firing.

The volunteer will fire 10 rounds in the order of file firing, and 10 in volleys, as detailed in the platoon exercise. The mark for these practices will be eight targets placed close together side by side, each having a separate bull's-eye and centre, of the dimensions detailed for the third class ; the distance to be 300 yards for file firing, and 400 yards for volley firing, if the range will admit.

Skirmishing.

Volunteers will fire 10 rounds in skirmishing order, both advancing and retiring between 200 and 400 yards. The marks for this practice to be eight targets placed in a row, each having a bull's-eye and circle, as for the third class, with intervals of six paces between them ; each file to have a separate target.

Registers of Firing.

The following registers will be kept by rifle corps. The forms may be obtained by application to the Secretary of State for War.

1. "*Target Practice Register,*" War Office Form 1601, in which the volunteers' names must be entered previously to going out to practise.

2. " *Musketry Drill and Practice Return,*" War Office Form 1600, which should be kept as a permanent register, in a book.

3. " *Table of performances in platoon and skirmishing* " *practices,*" War Office Form 1603, and on the back of Form 1600.

4. "Recapitulation," showing the figure of merit, to enable different corps to compare with each other, on back of Form 1600.

5. When trained instructors are employed, a *Judging Distance Register,* War Office Form 1602, may also be kept.

Marking Points and Classification.

The individual firing will be divided into three periods, 20 rounds to be fired in each.

In the first period each volunteer will fire five rounds at every distance of 50 yards, from 150 to 300 yards inclusive; the points gained will be marked in the "Target Practice " Register," Form 1600, and the total points obtained at each distance, will be transferred to "Musketry Drill and " Practice Return," Form 1600.

When the corps has completed the first period, the points obtained individually at the several distances, are to be added together, and the sum entered in the column "total " points" of the period, in the "Musketry Drill and Prac- " tice Return," Form 1600, to show the value of the per- formances of each volunteer, from which column a classi- fication is to be made ;—all those who have obtained 15 points and upwards, will fire the second period in the second class, and those who have not obtained this number, will fire their second period at the same distances as the first, that is, in the third class.

At the conclusion of the practices in the second period, the points obtained by each man at the several distances are to be added together, and the sum entered in the columns " total points," from which a second classification is to be made for the firing in the third period ; all men of the second class who have obtained 12 points and upwards, are to pass into the first class ; and all men of the third class, who have obtained 15 points and upwards, into the second class. Those men who have not obtained the number of points specified, will remain in the second and third classes respectively.

At the conclusion of the practices in the third period, the points obtained by each man are to be added together, and the sum entered in the columns " total points," from which a final classification is to be made, and entered in the columns for that purpose.

In file firing the bullets striking the target will have the same value, in points, as in the third class, and will be marked collectively in the Form 1603.

In volley firing the hits are to be counted as in the second class, bull's-eyes being reckoned only as centres.

In skirmishing the hits are to be counted as in volley firing ; bull's-eyes being only valued as centres.

The average points obtained in the " skirmishing prac-
" tice," and in the practices of "file and volley firing,"
added to the average obtained in the first period, will give
the " figure of merit " of the shooting of the corps.

The dates on which the preliminary drills are performed
will be entered in the " Musketry Drill and Practice
" Return."

W. O. Form 1601.

RIFLE VOLUNTEERS.

REGISTER of TARGET PRACTICE. Capt. _____ or _____ Company.

_____ Section. _____ Period. _____ Class. 18___

_____ Targets. Dated at _____

Distance: ___ Yards.								Distance: ___ Yards.						Yards.
Total Points.	Points obtained per Shot.					No. as per Practice Return.	Rank and Names.	Points obtained per Shot.					Total Points.
	5	4	3	2	1			1	2	3	4	5	
Totals.													Totals
Average.													Average

Instructor.

W. O. FORM 1600.

Captain_____'s, or

MUSKETRY DRILL and PRACTICE RETURN of the above Company for

Judging Distance Drills.						Snapping Caps and Blank Firing.		Position Drills.						Aiming Drills.						Theoretical Principles.			Cleaning of Arms.			Succession Number, agreeing with Practice Register.	RANK AND NAMES Of every Enrolled Member of the Company.	1ST PERIOD.					
																									Distances.				Total Points.	
																									150	200	250	300		150
PRELIMINARY DRILLS.																									Rounds.					
Least Number of Drills or Exercises to be performed by each Volunteer before he is to be allowed to proceed to Practice, specifying in the several Columns the Date when performed:—thus, 23/4.																									5	5	5	5		5
6	5	4	3	2	1	2	1	6	5	4	3	2	1	600 6	500 5	400 4	300 3	200 2	100 1	3	2	1	3	2	Points.					
																									1					
																									2					
																									3					
																									4					
																									5					
																									6					
																									7					
																									8					
																									9					
																									10					
																									11					
																									12					
																									13					
																									14					
																									15					
																									16					
																									17					
																									18					
																									19					
																									20					
																									21					
																									22					
																									23					
																									24					
																									25					
																									26					
																									27					
																									28					
																									29					
																									30					
																									&c.					
																								TOTALS						
																								AVERAGES - - -						

_____Instructor.

TARGET PRACTICES.

2ND PERIOD.									3RD PERIOD.																Final. Classification.			File Firing at 300 yards.	Volley Firing at 400 yards.	Skirmish between 400 and 200 yds.	REMARKS Showing the Date of ceasing to belong to the Company, and explaining the reason for the omission of the Training of those Volunteers not exercised.
3rd Class.				2nd Class.					3rd Class.					2nd Class.					1st Class.												
Distances.				Distances.					Distances.					Distances.					Distances.												* The figure 1 to be inserted opposite each Man's Name in one of the classification columns; and in each of the others when the practices are executed.
200	250	300		400	500	550	600		150	200	250	300		400	500	550	600		650	700	800	900									
Rounds.			Total Points.	Rounds.				Total Points.	Rounds.				Total Points.	Rounds.				Total Points.	Rounds.				Total Points.	Class.			Rounds.			
5	5	5		5	5	5	5		5	5	5	5		5	5	5	5		5	5	5	5		3d *	2d *	1st *	10 *	10 *	10 *	
Points.				Points.					Points.					Points.					Points.											

_Captain,_____

W. O. Form 1603 (for the Field) *and*
on back of W.O. Form 1600.

Captain_____, or_____ Company.

*County of*_____.

RIFLE VOLUNTEERS.

Form C, for use in the Field.

Table of Performances in Platoon and Skirmishing Practices.

Section, Squad, or Party.	File firing.			Volley firing.			Skirmishing.		
	No. of Men.	Total Points attained.	Average Points.	No. of Men.	Total Points attained.	Average Points.	No. of Men.	Total Points attained.	Average Points.
Total Men, Points, and Averages									

N.B.—Application to be made to War Office for fresh supply of these returns when required.

On back of W.O. Form 1600.

Recapitulation, showing the Merit of the Shooting of the Effective Men of the Volunteers on the_____ 18___ (the date to which Return is closed).

Average Points obtained in the 1st Period	-	-	-	-	
Do. do. in File firing	-	-	-	-	
Do. do. in Volley firing	-	-	-	-	
Do. do. in Skirmishing	-	-	-	-	
	Total, or "Figure of Merit."				

_____ Instructor.

Captain,_____

W. O. Form 1602.

Capt._____ _____ Company. _____ Section.

REGISTER OF JUDGING DISTANCE.

State of Atmosphere _____
Object _____
Dated at _____ 18__.

State of Atmosphere _____
Object _____
Dated at _____ 18__.

Total Points.	Correct Distances in Yards.											No. as per Practice Return.	RANK AND NAMES.	Correct Distances in Yards.												Total Points.
	Ans. 6	Pts.	Ans. 5	Pts.	Ans. 4	Pts.	Ans. 3	Pts.	Ans. 2	Pts.	Ans. 1	Pts.			Ans. 1	Pts.	Ans. 2	Pts.	Ans. 3	Pts.	Ans. 4	Pts.	Ans. 5	Pts.	Ans. 6	Pts.	

Totals. _____
Average. _____

Totals - - _____
Average - - _____

I CERTIFY that I was present during the performance of the Practice above recorded, which was conducted strictly in accordance with the Musketry Regulations, and that the answers given by each Man are those specified against his name.

_____ Instructor.

I CERTIFY that I was present during the performance of the Practice above recorded, which was conducted strictly in accordance with the Musketry Regulations, and that the answers given by each Man are those specified against his name.

_____ Instructor.

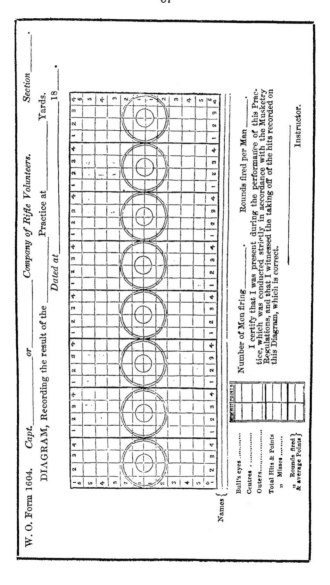

W. O. Form 1604.   *Capt.*   or   *Company of Rifle Volunteers.*   Section

DIAGRAM, Recording the result of the _____ Practice at _____ Yards.

Dated at _____ 18___.

Names

Number of Men firing _____.   Rounds fired per Man _____.

I certify that I was present during the performance of this Practice, which was conducted strictly in accordance with the Musketry Regulations, and that I witnessed the taking off of the hits recorded on this Diagram, which is correct.

Bull's eyes ....

Centres ....

Outers..................

Total Hits & Points

„ Misses ....

„ Rounds fired &
average Points

Instructor.

CIRCULAR

Promulgated by Order of the Secretary of State for War for the Guidance of Volunteer Rifle Corps.

War Office, 1st *September* 1859.

COURSE of RIFLE TRAINING for the VOLUNTEER RIFLE CORPS, supposed to train by Squads of 20 or 24 at a time, where two Instructors are available, or half these Numbers where there is only one.

PRELIMINARY DRILLS.

The Minimum Number of Drills, and Time to be employed in each, before Target Practice is on any account to commence.

Days.	Cleaning Arms.		Theoretical Principles.		Aiming Drill.		Position Drill per Musketry Regulations.	Snapping Caps. 10 Caps to be expended.	Blank Firing. 10 Rounds to be expended.	Judging Distance Drill.	Total Hours.
	Lessons per Musketry Regulations.	Time.	Lessons per Musketry Regulations.	Time.	Distance.	Time.					
		Hour.		Hour.	Yards.	Hour.	Hour.	Hour.	Hour.	Hour.	Hours.
1st	1st	½	–	–	100	½	¾	–	–	¾	2½
2nd	–	–	1 and 2	½	200	½	¾	–	–	¾	2½
3rd	3rd	½	–	–	300	½	¾	–	–	¾	2½
4th	–	–	3 and 4	½	400	½	¾	–	–	¾	2½
5th	4th	½	–	–	500	½	¼	½	–	¾	2½
6th	–	–	5 and 6	½	600	½	¼	–	½	¾	2½

TARGET PRACTICE.

Days.	Number of Rounds to be fired in												REMARKS.
	3rd Class.				2nd Class.				1st Class.				
	Yds. 150	Yds. 200	Yds 250	Yds. 300	Yds. 400	Yds. 500	Yds. 550	Yds. 600	Yds. 650	Yds. 700	Yds. 800	Yds. 900	
7th	5	5	–	–	–	–	–	–	–	–	–	–	1st Period.
8th	–	–	5	5	–	–	–	–	–	–	–	–	
9th	5	5	–	–	5	5	–	–	–	–	–	–	2nd Period — 3rd Class to fire from 150 to 300 yards; 2nd Class from 400 to 600 yards.
10th	–	–	5	5	–	–	5	5	–	–	–	–	
11th	5	5	–	–	5	5	–	–	5	5	–	–	3rd Period — 3rd and 2nd Class to fire as before; 1st Class from 650 to 900 yards.
12th	–	–	5	–	–	–	5	5	–	–	5	5	

P.S.—Should it be desirable to execute the Platoon and Skirmishing Practices, two more days will be required for the purpose, viz., 13th day, File-firing at 300 yards, standing, 10 rounds; Volley-firing at 400 yards, kneeling, 10 rounds. 14th day, Skirmishing, Advancing, and Retiring (each man judging his own distance), between 400 and 200 yards, 10 rounds.

LONDON: Printed by GEORGE E. EYRE and WILLIAM SPOTTISWOODE, Printers to the Queen's most Excellent Majesty.

For Her Majesty's Stationery Office.